California Theme Parks

GIANT DIPPER
SAN DIEGO
ON
Ride Photos

California Theme Parks

Alex Miller and Bryce Walker

Schiffer® Publishing Ltd

4880 Lower Valley Road, Atglen, Pennsylvania 19310

Other Schiffer Books on Related Subjects:
Wildwood, Neon Nights & Motel Memories, Robert O. and Melinda M. Williams
Las Vegas Lights, Mark P. and Robert Block

Library of Congress Control Number: 2010921712

Designed by Mark David Bowyer
Type set in Aldine721 BT / Zurich BT

ISBN: 978-07643-3478-8
Printed in China

Schiffer Books are available at special discounts for bulk purchases for sales promotions or premiums. Special editions, including personalized covers, corporate imprints, and excerpts can be created in large quantities for special needs. For more information contact the publisher:

Published by Schiffer Publishing Ltd.
4880 Lower Valley Road
Atglen, PA 19310
Phone: (610) 593-1777; Fax: (610) 593-2002
E-mail: Info@schifferbooks.com

For the largest selection of fine reference books on this and related subjects, please visit our web site at **www.schifferbooks.com**
We are always looking for people to write books on new and related subjects. If you have an idea for a book please contact us at the above address.

This book may be purchased from the publisher.
Include $5.00 for shipping.
Please try your bookstore first.
You may write for a free catalog.

In Europe, Schiffer books are distributed by
Bushwood Books
6 Marksbury Ave.
Kew Gardens
Surrey TW9 4JF England
Phone: 44 (0) 20 8392 8585; Fax: 44 (0) 20 8392 9876
E-mail: info@bushwoodbooks.co.uk
Website: www.bushwoodbooks.co.uk

Dedication

This book is dedicated to
James and Laura Miller
and everyone who hasn't yet let the
curtain fall on their childhood memories.

Contents

1

2

3

4

5

6

7

8

9

10

11

12

13

14

15

16

17

18

19

20

Acknowledgments

An idea can often be traced back to one person, but without the support of countless others, it would likely die in the same brain that conceived it. Our book was no different. Without the help of many others, this book would never have come to fruition.

First, I thank Laura Miller for painstakingly editing this text before I passed it along to the publisher. Next, I acknowledge Brigid Fuller, who made the process so much easier. Without her intricate knowledge of the publishing process and amusement park publicity, this book would never have been completed. Special thanks goes to Charles Canfield, who wrote the Foreword and is the most knowledgeable person I know about the amusement park industry, and talented artist Caroline Miller.

Behind the scenes, we acknowledge the following people who helped to make the book a reality: Hanna Kim, Lucia Worthington, James Miller, Pam Ranta, Ken Germann, Renee and Shane Walker, Greg Walther, and Evan Ranta, the book's vice-president of hospitality and lodging/assistant water-boy.

Additionally, we thank the following park representatives. Whether they gave personalized tours, provided "little known secrets" of their park, or granted the use of certain images, each played a supportive role: Allen Ansdell Jr., Mr. and Mrs. Allen Ansdell Sr., Wendy Crain, Randal Metz, Margaret Adamic, Sam Johnston, Meghan Gardener, Michael Minicilli, Julie Estrada, Jeff Klocke, Barry Falke, Connie Rojas, Robert Couey, Nancy Chan, Sue Carpenter, and Audrey Eig.

Finally, special thanks is given to everyone at Schiffer Publishing for giving our "amusement park book" a chance.

Foreword

Alex Miller's keen interest in amusement parks inspired him to research and write this book on California amusement parks, large and small, scattered around the Golden State.

Alex worked at the Santa Cruz Beach Boardwalk for two seasons while attending the University of California, Santa Cruz. While working here, Alex would come by my office and talk about amusement parks and what makes them so special. We both agreed that people want a safe place where they can escape from their everyday environment and just have fun with their friends and family. And older folks enjoy sharing memories of their youth spent in such places. People never forget their first ride on a carousel, winning their first prize, or taking that first plunge down a steep hill on a thrilling coaster.

Recognizing nostalgia as an important part of the amusement park experience. Alex wondered how the Boardwalk managed to keep the feel of an authentic seaside amusement park while introducing modern rides and equipment. I believe a large part of our park's charm is that we have never forgotten our beginnings. Over the years, the Boardwalk has collected antiques from other amusement parks as well as saved our own. We have preserved what we consider a real American experience.

Alex's genuine enthusiasm for his subject provides the reader with a fresh look at California amusement parks, which are as diverse and interesting as the state itself. This book should be a useful guide, no matter what your age. Because even as we grow older, there is still a little child left in us all.

—Charles Canfield
President, Santa Cruz Beach Boardwalk

Introduction

I have a great job.

Okay, even that's an understatement. As a student with one year left in college, it became my job to travel to amusement parks throughout California, with my photographer-friend Bryce, to ride the rides, eat the food, learn the history, and to understand and experience every unique park. It was a labor of love. From the beaches of San Diego to the state capitol, our quest to discover each unique park was also a tribute to the world of theme parks.

For over a century, amusement parks have spanned the Golden State. They first appeared along the beaches, multiplying along the coastline and igniting an industry that has grown and seen tremendous change and innovation. Today, only three "Golden Age" seaside parks remain in California, and these patriarchal treasures are recognized for their history and nostalgic charm. Since the early days, California's theme parks have transformed the world of entertainment and family fun. Creations like Knott's Berry Farm and Children's Fairyland—America's first theme park and first children's theme park, respectively—have set high standards for the entire world. They and others that followed introduced some of the most innovative ideas entertainment has ever seen. With the opening of Disneyland in 1955, amusement parks became destinations in themselves, transforming surrounding communities.

Theme parks make people happy. Like many kids, I grew up visiting these magical places and consider them a staple of my childhood. There is something incredibly fulfilling about them; they are wholesome family entertainment, a setting for budding romance, and a place to recall the past with joy. Among the many "firsts" that fill our photo albums are the first merry-go-round rides, and we all recall the mixed anticipation, excitement, and dread of our first roller coaster. These are enchanting experiences and memories that never grow old.

I remember watching a carousel late one summer evening, listening to the music and enjoying the energy and happiness I felt around me. The antique organ was playing the same song it had cranked out for over a century, while multi-colored lights danced above the carousel's carefully preserved, hand-painted artwork. Some children were waiting for their first ride ever and the anticipation in their eyes was endearing. People around me were laughing and eating cotton candy and hot dogs. Suddenly, a gray-haired couple, giggling and breathless with excitement, came running past the bench where I sat. The sight was common enough, but the euphoric feeling was what I held onto.

In writing this book, I met with countless theme park owners and even employees who have been with their parks for more than 50 years... and you know what? They couldn't be happier. You see them every day roaming their park before it opens like it was their own backyard—recounting each memory, reliving each moment. They genuinely take pride in their work and couldn't be happier to call their park a second home.

That's what an amusement park is: a happy place, a dwelling of carefree youth and bliss that is temporarily removed from the real world. Whether one visits with family, friends, a sweetheart, or even alone, the experience brightens your mood and lifts your spirits.

I'm a bit of a traditionalist when it comes to theme parks. I enjoy the latest and the greatest but will always have a soft spot for the parks and rides that started everything. That is what this book is all about. It is a snapshot of California's parks today, but also pays homage to how they began and how they have evolved over time (see the Timeline on pages 126 and 127).

California is truly the theme park Mecca of the world. With twenty highly diverse parks for guests of all ages, there has never been such an abundance of entertainment possibility. In dedicating Disneyland, Walt Disney said, "Here age relives fond memories of the past... and here youth may savor the challenge and promise of the future." In a prophetic way, these words echo through every park where memories are made daily and the innovation is never-ending.

Now come and experience each one—the fantasy, the possibility, and the timeless happiness of each theme park in the Golden State.

1 Adventure City

Stanton, California

When it comes to great theme parks, no place in the world compares to Southern California. The world's most iconic and extravagant adventures await guests, all within about a two hour driving radius, from the beaches of San Diego to the mountains of Valencia. At the heart of it all lie the Disneyland Resort in Anaheim and Knott's Berry Farm in Buena Park. Just 10 minutes between these two mega parks is Adventure City. Built in 1994, this delightful park has been flourishing despite the impressive shadows cast by its closest neighbors.

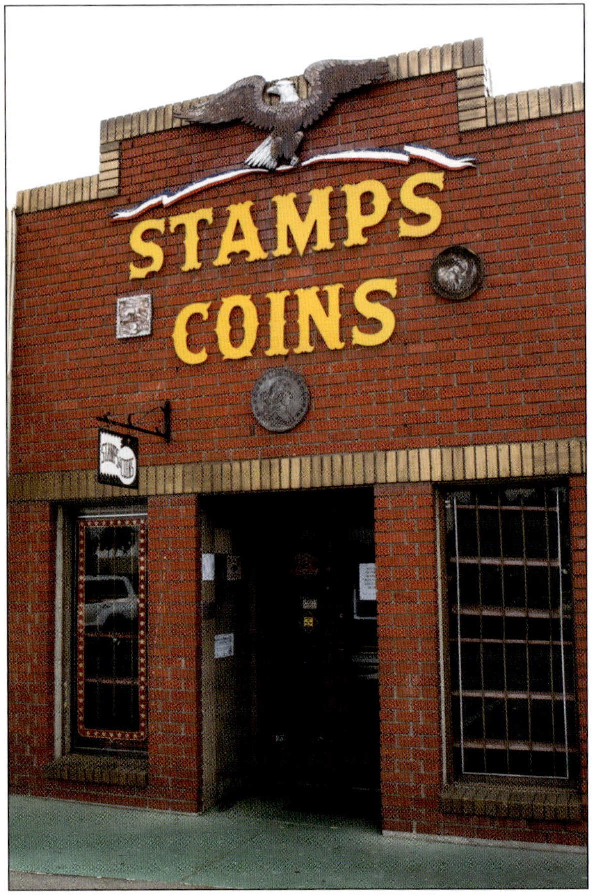

One of many specialty collector shops in Hobby City, the mother of Adventure City.

When Disneyland opened its gates in 1955, a couple, Bea and Jay DeArmond, purchased a six-acre chicken ranch on Beach Boulevard with the dream of creating a one-stop hobby and collector center featuring unique stores found nowhere else. That dream was quickly realized and "Hobby City" was born. In 1965, a small, vintage-1938, express train was added to give visitors rides during their visit to the distinctive shopping center. For three and a half decades, Hobby City prospered, just as the DeArmond's had envisioned it would. Then, in 1989, change came about.

Railroad tracks for the park's first ride, the vintage "Adventure City Express Train," circle the park. The 70-year-old attraction could not find a better home than Hobby City/Adventure City.

Consistent with the park's theme, even the strollers are designed to blend into the little city. Single children may take a taxi around the park while siblings drive around in a fire truck.

Despite the convenience and renown of Southern California's largest and most famous theme parks, some local families found the prices out of reach. The idea of spending hundreds for a day at one of the big-name parks just wasn't a feasible option, so plans for a more affordable park were drawn up by the DeArmond's grandson, Allen Ansdell Jr. With the help of his family and the purchase of adjacent property, Adventure City opened right next to Hobby City five years later, catering to families with young children. Admission for a family of four to Adventure City was roughly the same price as one ticket to any of the larger parks.

From outside the park, the "Party Tree House" is easily the most distinguishable facet of the park.

Inside the "Party Tree House," children are welcomed to an intricately themed area for birthday festivities. Just like Walt Disney's apartment above the Fire Station on Main Street at Disneyland Park, the Ansdell's maintain an in-park apartment on the second story of the "Party Tree House."

As the name suggests, the park is a child-friendly city. A miniature airport, train station, and police and fireman station with authentic uniforms for the children all play into the imaginative and charming façade. Two birthday party rooms, themed and decorated with incredible attention to detail, help make any child's special day one to remember for years to come.

One of the birthday party rooms features a shady boulevard with birthday presents "delivered by taxi." On the very right hand side, the "Adventure City Express Train" makes a visit every few minutes through a tunnel in the party room.

"Rescue 911" allows children to not only dress up and drive around in real fire-fighter and policeman gear, but also respond to humorous emergency calls over the intercom.

Before boarding one of Adventure City's two flying attractions, "Balloon Ride" and "Barnstormer Planes," children and parents await their flight in the Adventure City terminal.

With eleven rides, including a family coaster, Wild mouse coaster, and a free-fall tower, the park proudly accommodates families with children of any age, while a petting farm, arcade, children's theater, and rock climbing wall help extend the amusement beyond the rides. As a tribute to its start with Hobby City, Adventure City also offers a children's model train area with one of the world's largest collections of wooden railways, reassembled in new ways every day by the excited children who visit the park.

Adventure City has done well in a very competitive location. With such a friendly family atmosphere, this intimate little park has a lot going for it. A small treasure among giants, maybe this little city—like Hobby City—is one of those unique places found nowhere else in the world.

A perfect ride for both children and adults, "Balloon Ride" passengers will soon be airborne, twenty-five feet above the city.

The "Tree Top Racers" are Adventure City's most thrilling ride. The classic, wild-mouse coaster gives guests a wonderful bird's-eye view of the park, while incorporating tight turns and sizeable drops throughout.

The "Petting Farm" offers a variety of docile animals including rabbits, chicks, and sheep.

They said it couldn't be done, but somehow the family "Freeway Coaster" found its way up, over, and through the branches of a giant pepper tree.

2 Belmont Park

San Diego, California

Along with the Santa Cruz Beach Boardwalk and Pacific Park, Belmont Park is one of the last reminders of a time in the 1920s that many people refer to as the "Golden Age" of amusement parks. There was a time across the state of California when seaside parks dominated the landscape of the coast. They weren't just a destination, but a way of life—a carefree beckoning to everyone for California sun and amusement. For many seaside parks that act closed and moved on a long time ago, as the state and industry moved on to bigger things. However, for three enduring landmarks the curtain has not yet fallen; Belmont Park, one of the remaining three, is still in an encore decades later.

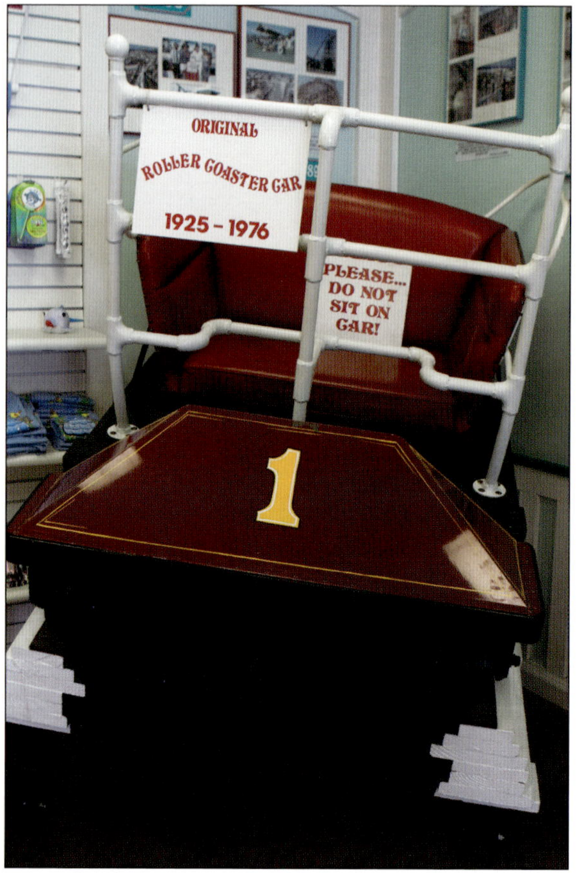

One of the original "Giant Dipper" roller coaster cars is still available for viewing at the museum.

For roller coaster history buffs, more information about the "Giant Dipper" landmark can be found at the park's miniature roller coaster museum.

Through the years, the "Giant Dipper" roller coaster has been threatened with demolition, but it continues to offer thrilling rides over the San Diego beach, just as it did in 1925. Now, as a National Historic Landmark, it will remain a treasure for future generations of beach-goers to experience and enjoy.

The legacy of Belmont Park—or the Mission Beach Amusement Center—began in 1925. With a bath house, skating rinks, and a roller coaster, it wasn't long before the seaside park wore its way into the hearts of many San Diegans. The Giant Dipper, a 1925 wooden roller coaster that shares its name with the 1924 coaster at the Santa Cruz Beach Boardwalk, proved to be an instant classic as visitors lined up for hours for a ride over the San Diego Beach. The park's charm and charisma carried it through decades, as sailors stationed at the nearby Navy Base found the park a popular attraction before shipping out during World War II. As owners changed through the years, the park saw modifications as well. A few more rides were added along with miniature golf and other attractions. Finally, in 1976, after half a century of entertainment and unparalleled growth, the park owner announced that due to rising costs, the park would not reopen the following year.

The "Pirates of Belmont" attraction features both black light miniature golfing as well as a state-of-the-art video arcade.

Inside the "Pirates of Belmont" attraction.

A series of untimely fires decimated the park and neglect turned public sentiment against it. By the early 1980s, demolition seemed imminent for this once-popular California landmark, which had become an eyesore. Luckily, in 1982, the Giant Dipper roller coaster was donated to a roller coaster preservation committee and, with help from the American Coaster Enthusiasts, it and the park were restored to their former glory five years later and designated a Historical Landmark. Currently, the Santa Cruz Seaside Company and Santa Cruz Beach Boardwalk oversee much of Belmont Park's activity and ensure that it stays a proud monument to the Golden Age of seaside parks.

Appropriately named, the "Liberty Carousel" is one of many classic attractions that no seaside park would be complete without. All of the carousel's artwork is patterned after photos preserved by the San Diego Historical Society.

Ten rides make up the ocean park today, which is still the ending destination for many San Diego beach-goers. Bumper cars and a classic Tilt-A-Whirl ride pay homage to Belmont Park's proud seaside roots while the new "Beach Blaster" ride and "Laser Maze Challenge" have brought new thrills and entertainment to the park.

Belmont Park offers a wide selection of beach gear from a variety of shops. Puka shell and shark teeth necklaces are among the popular accessories for sale.

One of many other classic seaside park rides, "Chaos" can be found alongside the "Giant Dipper" roller coaster.

Starfish, sand dollars, and every type of shell imaginable can be found for sale at the beachfront park's souvenir shops.

Anyone searching for a true Southern California experience will find it at Belmont Park. The nation's first amusement park to feature the "FlowRider®," an endless simulated wave attraction, Belmont Park offers the best of the laid-back surfing culture. Talk of building a state-of-the-art surfing reef and possible water park is on the horizon. Regardless, this famed destination has proven itself a timeless landmark of the Golden State.

The "Wave House®" at Belmont Park is home to the "Flow Rider®" attraction, and remains very popular during the summer due in part to San Diego's strong surfing culture.

In addition to classic bumper cars, Belmont Park also features "Krazy Kars," a flying saucer-type take on the seaside park favorite.

A typical outdoor souvenir stand at Belmont Park.

3 California's Great America

Santa Clara, California

Born on our nation's 200th birthday, California's Great America has been entertaining theme park enthusiasts with an arsenal of continued innovation since its opening in 1976. This Bicentennial park provides a constant and sometimes not-quite-so-subtle reminder of our nation's proud history with its patriotic theme. The first steps through the gate open onto *Celebration Plaza*, with extravagant fountains, an ensemble of American Flags, a miniature Mt. Rushmore replica, and the world's tallest double-decker carousel—painted for the occasion in robust red, white, and blue. The multi-storied carousel's spire stretches resoundingly toward the sky suggesting to dazzled guests what they can expect from the rest of the park: an American experience with the best of thrills.

Subtle paint jobs throughout pay tribute to the park's Americana theme. Notice that when the blue log flume is lined up with the red and white striped lighthouse, it gives the effect of a backward American flag.

"Vortex," a standing roller coaster, prepares thrill-seekers for an incredible ride.

From flowers to signs, as soon as guests pass through the turnstiles they find a consistent color scheme of red, white, and blue throughout the park.

In 1983, California's Great America first made history with the introduction of "The Edge," one of the first free-fall rides in the world. Though it was taken out in the late 1980s, it was replaced in 1996 with "Drop Tower Scream Zone," a 224-foot free-fall tower that reaches speeds around 62 miles per hour. The park also lays claim to the invention of an entirely new concept of coaster. In 2006, California's Great America introduced "SURVIVOR The Ride" as the world's first reality-themed coaster. The experience begins in the queue line, where guests are divided into tribes and challenged to a tribal noise-making contest before boarding a revolving disc on the coaster track. Based on their performance in the queue, the coaster rotates as tiki men spray water and hot air to those on the ride. Those who performed worst in the queue emerge wet from the experience.

Tribes compete to outplay, outwit and outlast their competition on "SURVIVOR: The Ride."

The popular "Drop Tower Scream Zone" lifts guests slowly into the air and holds them at the top of the tower for several seconds before hurtling them back to the ground.

The park offers eight different roller coasters, from the "Rugrats Runaway Reptar" family coaster to sprawling, suspended, standing, steel, and wooden coasters, each with its own allure. In addition, a large variety of water rides and a brand new adjacent waterpark beckon as a means to cool off as the afternoon heats up. Kiddie-themed lands like *Nickelodeon™ Central* and *Kidzville®* ensure that there is something to entertain everyone regardless of age or height. Family friendly shows and classic carnival games cap off the experience nicely, inviting guests to enjoy more than just the stellar array of rides offered throughout the park.

The appropriately named "Psycho Mouse" is a wild mouse coaster suitable for both children and adults.

Guests would be best advised to bring a swim suit to enjoy California's Great America. With complementary admission to the sizable *Boomerang Bay* water park, guests can enjoy both water slides and roller coasters during their visit and pay only one price.

All over the park, guests find roller coasters weaving in, out, and around the land, through the treetops, and even over a lake.

The "Eagle's Flight" offers a rapid—though scenic—way to get from one side of the park to the other. Below, California's Great America merges with *Boomerang Bay* at the "Kookaburra Cay" water play area.

California's Great America offers a family-friendly environment that is big on thrills and action-packed rides. With talk of greater thrills on the horizon, California's Great America maintains its reputation as a leader of invention when it comes to new ways to excite the theme-park fanatic.

The theme park in general has always embodied a feel-good American experience. Great America's patriotic theme, grandeur, and extravagance push it into the limelight as a park that sincerely lives up to its name. One can only wonder what will be next for this park, as it continues to create in the true spirit of American competition.

"Flight Deck" is one of Great America's most popular roller coasters.

"Invertigo" features a well-known coaster track but was the first roller coaster in North America to seat its riders face-to-face instead of all in one direction.

The spire of "Carousel Columbia" reaches even higher than its neighboring roller coasters. At ten stories, this world's tallest carousel has been a park icon since it opened with Great America in 1976.

4

Castle Park

Riverside, California

As California's eastern-most amusement park, Castle Park is sometimes overlooked by tourists heading toward the coast. This beautifully landscaped family park offers an abundance of rides and other attractions, including multiple family coasters, a vertical launch tower, and a log flume. Castle Park's claim to fame, however, isn't its location or its rides, but its fabulous miniature golf courses.

Boasting four 18-hole miniature golf courses that have been featured in televised tournaments, Castle Park offers challenges for every skill level from beginner to professional. Eighteen waterfalls grace the beautiful courses, and each hole is extravagantly themed. Standing in the center of the four courses and gazing out in any direction, the effect is almost overwhelming; this is a true mini-golfers paradise with new and exciting courses in every direction, almost as far as the eye can see. Themes of each hole range from castles around the world to Candyland to the Old West. The abundance of playing options are enough to keep any mini-golfer intrigued and entertained for the better part of their visit to this unique park.

A golf course hole themed to the Old West.

In addition to simply circling the park, the "Castle Park Railroad" also cuts through it, giving a peaceful yet comprehensive tour of each of the thirty-five rides and attractions offered, making it a great way to begin any guest's stay.

A gingerbread house golf course hole.

Standing in the center of all four golf courses creates a mesmerizing effect, due to the range of playing options.

Due to its prestigious mini-golf courses, it comes as no surprise that when Castle Park opened in 1976 it offered only the golf courses alongside a large arcade. It wasn't until 1985, with the addition of rides, that it began its transformation into the unique park it is today. With four coasters including a new spinning coaster, thrills are now an essential part of the family fun that Castle Park offers all its guests. Nostalgia however, also has its place; located in the center of all the fun stands an early 1900s Dentzel Carousel surrounded by beautiful in-house paintings and antique carousel horses.

The Dentzel Carousel, simply called "Merry-Go-Round" by the park, features a beautiful menagerie of animals in addition to the usual carousel horses.

Strategically placed billboard-size maps throughout the park offer an easy glimpse of where a guest's next attraction lies.

Also brought back from the past is a collection of authentic 18th century mining equipment that now proudly adorns the "Gold Rush" themed trains and creates interest along the perimeter of the log ride. Not all scenery garnishing the rides is Western themed however. In fact the majority of the park's ornamentation pays tribute to its medieval sounding roots. "Merlin's Revenge," the park's most prominent coaster, welcomes visitors at the main entrance with a statue of the wizard from King Arthur's days. This coaster and the famous medieval themed carousel guide the way to the park's largest and most striking symbol, an ornate castle at the far end of the park. Inside, the castle offers an enormous arcade and the newest dark ride, "Ghost Blasters." A family shooting attraction, guests embark together on a quest to rid the castle of pesky ghosts.

During the summer months, Riverside California can get up to 110°F, so the "Log Ride" offers a very welcome opportunity for guests to cool-off in the mid-afternoon.

Inside the park's namesake castle, visitors travel through spooky corridors armed with laser guns. Each ghost "blasted" earns points for its shooter.

Like almost all of Castle Park's attractions, "Merlin's Revenge" is a coaster suitable for all ages.

Though Castle Park has many rides, its close attention to detail and rich themes make this a family fun zone always worthy of a visit. A family-friendly atmosphere coupled with the Pebble Beach of miniature golf courses, Castle Park is a hole-in-one.

Waterfalls and intricate scenery will draw the attention of every mini-golfer.

For mini-golf fanatics, the park offers enough different courses to keep any guest entertained for the day, even without rides.

Opposite Page:
"King's Crown," a classic swing attraction, offers a bird's-eye view of the park.

5 Children's Fairyland

Oakland, California

Oakland, California, has the urban vibe of any large city, surrounded by busy freeways and an abundance of office buildings. Entering the city, one would never guess that Oakland is also home one of the most famous and endearing children's parks in the world. Children's Fairyland was the first park with an over-arching theme to cater exclusively to young children, and has since been copied and used as a model for many other prominent theme parks around the globe.

Children's Fairyland was conceived in 1950 by an Oakland nurseryman, Arthur Navlet. On a trip to Detroit, he was inspired by a collection of small nursery rhyme buildings and wanted to create life-size duplicates that children could play in. Once back in Oakland, with the help of the Lake Merritt Breakfast Club and Oakland Park Superintendent William Penn Mott, they hired an architect, William Russell Everritt, to design seventeen storybook sets at a child's eye level. When Everritt had completed the first small building, Mott took a look at it and told him it was too staid and not quite what he was looking for. Not discouraged in the least, Everritt happily took a hammer to the set and destroyed it. Redrawing his plans entirely, Everritt built the next set with no straight sides and added vibrant colors and textures. Mott was delighted with the cartoon-like structure, and the whimsical look of Children's Fairyland was born.

Though parents can enjoy the park with their kids, the park's name offers an enlightening clue as to who Children's Fairyland was really built for.

"Anansi's Magic Web" Ferris wheel is one of the park's four children's rides.

Rapunzel glances out of the tower window at one of Everritt's many storybook sets

Since it opened, children have always visited "The Old Lady in the Shoe" before entering the park.

In addition to serving as a model for children's parks across the world, Children's Fairyland can also lay claim with the oldest continuously operating puppet theater in the nation. The park features classic puppet shows daily, from children's fairytales and nursery rhymes. The puppet theater has had a number of great talents get their start performing here, including Frank Oz, who went on to play and voice puppet characters such as Miss Piggy, Cookie Monster, and Yoda.

Since 1956, the Storybook Puppet Theater has entertained millions of delighted children.

Children's Fairyland has seen its fair share of news media coverage, including a time when Walt Disney visited in the early 1950s looking for inspiration for Disneyland. Many people argue that Children's Fairyland served an important role in Walt Disney's development of Disneyland and was a prime example to him that, if built correctly like Fairyland, a children's park could be just as successful, if not more so, than the typical amusement park of the day. Bruce Sedley, an Oakland television personality, also made frequent appearances at the park and would recite the stories of each Fairyland set. Because, over time, his voice couldn't take the daily storytelling, he invented a system of talking books with recorded stories activated by a key—a system that is still used extensively in amusement parks and zoos around the world today.

For guests paying close attention, some sets appear similar to those at Disneyland. When he visited, Walt Disney was very impressed with Children's Fairyland and credited it as one of his park's major inspirations.

Guests of all ages are invited "down the rabbit hole" to help Alice search for the elusive white rabbit.

Bruce Sedley's famous talking storybook and magic key system, invented in Children's Fairyland, now offers children who visit the park the opportunity to hear stories in both English and Spanish.

The park offers storytellers, magicians, live animals, and entertainment provided by local children as well as a brand new Greek-style amphitheater featuring Aesop's fables. Every plant, every animal, every set in the park serves the overarching theme about the wonders of childhood and the importance of growing imaginations. It is the irreplaceable children's theme park that started it all.

Perhaps one reason Children's Fairyland remains so popular is that it incorporates fairytales from every corner of the globe. European-, American-, and Asian-themed areas can be found throughout the park. This set, themed to Anansi the Spider, is a popular West African story.

Fairyland's popularity has attracted more than English speaking guests; thus it offers multi-lingual signs as well as park maps printed in three languages. The organic garden, also seen here, is harvested to feed all the park's petting zoo animals.

"Aesop's Playhouse" provides a spectacular venue for local children to put on performances.

What better words could end a child's day after their visit to a fairytale town?

6 Disneyland Park
Anaheim, California

Disneyland—"The Happiest Place on Earth"—may be the most loved and famous theme park in the world. Since its opening in 1955, Disneyland has enchanted millions each year as one of the most visited destinations in the world.

Disneyland was a dream years in the making. Walt Disney saw the need for a family-friendly park and originally had envisioned a place with a few trains, stagecoaches, and boats for his employees and visitors to his animations studios; in time, however, Walt's dream—skeptics called it "Walt's Folly"—had become truly spectacular. When it opened and enjoyed wild success, Disneyland set a new standard for the industry and all future imitators, redefining the possibilities of amusement parks and family entertainment.

For more than a half century, Sleeping Beauty Castle has served as a gateway to fantasy and imagination at Disneyland Park. © Disney Enterprises, Inc.

Among the many entertainment firsts achieved by Walt Disney Imagineering was the invention of "Audio-Animatronics"—or robots that could both move and talk for guests. Abraham Lincoln has been entertaining and inspiring at Disneyland Park since the mid-1960s and was one of the first Audio-Animatronics characters created. © Disney Enterprises, Inc.

From fantasy to future and mountain peaks to ocean floors, Disneyland Park has always sought to bridge the thin gap between imagination and reality. © Disney Enterprises, Inc.

On its opening day, July 17th, 1955, Disneyland offered five themed lands that immersed guests in unique settings. *Main Street, USA* was based on Walt Disney's own hometown in the early 1900s, Marceline, Missouri, and has remained virtually unchanged since the park's opening. *Adventureland* features exotic travel attractions and a dense jungle now aged to perfection over 50 years, while *Frontierland* depicts pioneer days of the Old West. *Fantasyland* is a colorful storybookland based on fairytale characters and children's stories, and *Tomorrowland*, originally built during the "space race" of the 1950s, has continued to reinvent itself as it imagines the world of the future. Walt Disney promised that Disneyland would never be finished, and over the years it has continued to grow, with the addition of *New Orleans Square*, *Critter Country*, and *Mickey's Toontown*.

"it's a small world" features singing children from around the world. It quickly became one of Disneyland Park's most famous attractions, when it opened in 1966. In 2009, Disney characters also found a new home in the ride. Alice and the White Rabbit, two of the ride's new characters, can be found in England. © Disney Enterprises, Inc.

Since it opened in 1955, "Jungle Cruise" has taken adventure-seekers on a one-of-a-kind excursion to the far regions of the globe. © Disney Enterprises, Inc.

For inquisitive guests, "Innoventions" offers a glimpse of goods that will improve the lives of tomorrow. © Disney Enterprises, Inc.

Disneyland has been called the first modern theme park. Walt regarded each day in the park as a show, calling employees "cast members" who were to treat visitors as guests. He insisted on perfect cleanliness, beautiful landscaping, and even made waiting in line entertaining, with queues helping the guest anticipate the ride. The park inspired books, movics, and even had its own television show.

For decades, Disneyland Park created rides from its own hit movies. However, "Pirates of the Caribbean" worked in reverse, turning a popular ride into numerous box-office hits. © Disney Enterprises, Inc.

Inspired by the feature films, "Indiana Jones Adventure" boasts astounding special effects and an incredibly detailed queue, complete with booby traps. © Disney/Lucasfilm Ltd.

Disneyland's "Imagineers" have kept the park's attractions fresh and exciting, allowing visitors to become, for a day, jungle explorers, bobsled racers, space voyagers, kings and queens, and even children. "Space Mountain" and "Star Tours," both imaginative firsts when they opened, whirl riders through outer space, while the log flume, "Splash Mountain," drops visitors in search of a "laughing place" into bayous of the Old South and the Uncle Remus folk tales. "it's a small world" celebrates children around the globe, while "Indiana Jones" takes adventurers on a quest into the Temple of the Forbidden Eye. Bobsledders zip around the Matterhorn, evading the legendary abominable snowman, while "Dumbo," "Peter Pan's Flight," "Storybook Land Canal Boats," and "Mr. Toad's Wild Ride" offer a gentle experience for the little ones. A true one-of-a-kind park that continues to astound and provide a lifetime of memories, this may truly be the one place in the world where imagination and laughter supercede age. It is a place where even Great-grandpa is still a child at heart.

Narrowly escaping the clutches of Br'er Fox and Br'er Bear, guests are sent hurtling into the briar patch on "Splash Mountain." © Disney Enterprises, Inc.

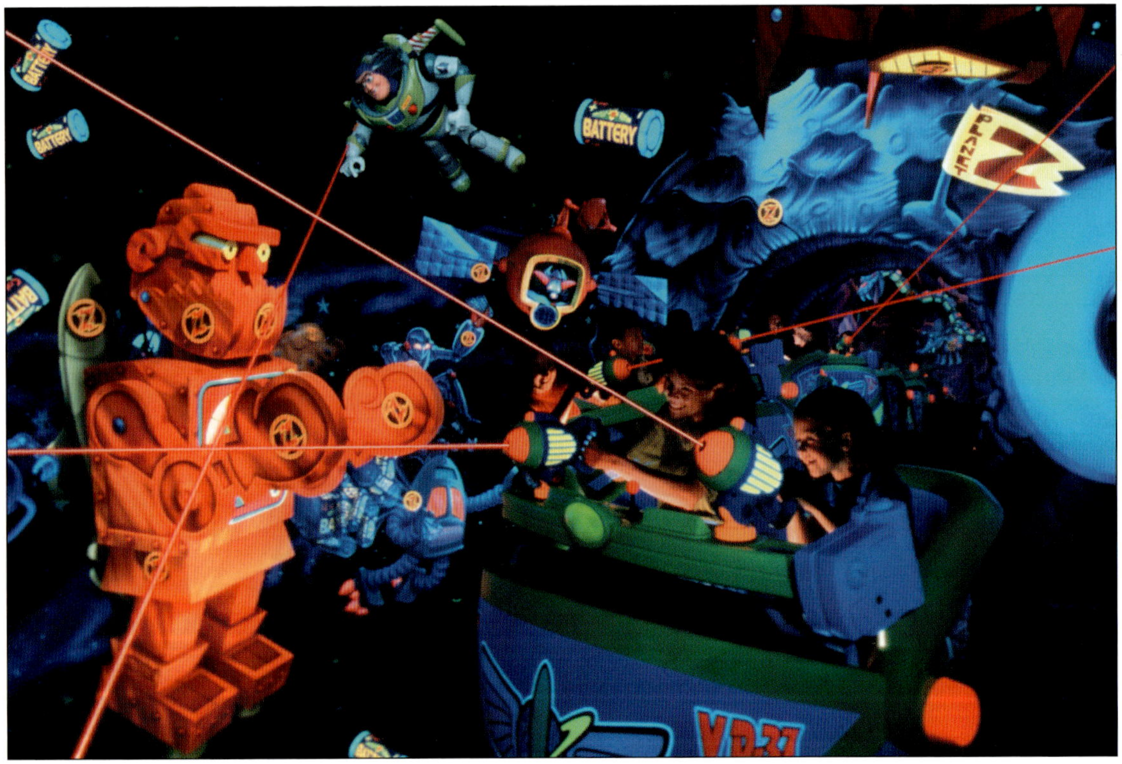

"Buzz Lightyear Astro Blasters" is a shooting attraction where honorary space rangers join Buzz to recover the "crystallic fusion cells" stolen by the Evil Emporer Zurg. © Disney Enterprises, Inc./Pixar

Guests with some daring and nerve may wish to visit the 999 happy haunts currently residing in the "Haunted Mansion," but there is always room for one more should they choose to stay © Disney Enterprises, Inc.

Sometimes it doesn't take much to find the child in everyone. © Disney Enterprises, Inc.

7 Disney's California Adventure Park

Anaheim, California

Talk of a second Disney Park in Southern California began roughly a decade before Disney's California Adventure opened on February 8th, 2001. Originally, The Walt Disney Company had planned to open a park called "WestCOT," a fresh interpretation of the Epcot Center at the Walt Disney World Resort near Orlando, Florida. It was planned to add nightlife to the Disneyland Resort in Anaheim, and for the first time feature "in-the-park" hotels for guests to remain immersed in the Disney experience. Various reasons eventually prevented "WestCOT" from coming to fruition, but by 1998 The Walt Disney Company finally broke ground for the construction of a long-anticipated Disneyland sister-park, Disney's California Adventure. After Disneyland Park, Disney's California Adventure is the second most visited park in the state.

As the Disneyland Resort expanded to accommodate Disney's California Adventure Park, two new hotels were also added. Disney's Grand Californian Hotel and Spa opened inside Disney's California Adventure Park, fulfilling the dream of an "in-the-park" hotel. © Disney Enterprises, Inc.

Guests found a whole new park filled with thrills when Disney's California Adventure Park opened in 2001. © Disney Enterprises, Inc.

The original entrance to Disney's California Adventure Park was "Imagineered" to look like a postcard, welcoming guests to all the best California had to offer. © Disney Enterprises, Inc.

Geared toward a more adult audience with fine dining, wine tasting, and an abundance of thrill rides, California Adventure opened with three major lands. *Hollywood Pictures Backlot* pays homage to California's entertainment industry and features movie-themed attractions, while *Paradise Pier* offers the nostalgic feel of the once so emblematic seaside parks the spanned the coast during the "Golden Age" of amusement parks. *The Golden State* land invites guests to experience and explore the natural beauty of California from vineyards to redwoods and in 2003, *A Bug's Land* opened for the youngest crowd and provides attractions based off the popular Disney/Pixar film.

Disney's California Adventure Park proudly offers a variety of exquisite dining options. © Disney Enterprises, Inc.

To satisfy the tastes of a more adult audience, Disney's California Adventure Park offers informative wine experts for those wishing to relax and partake in the Terrace Wine Tasting. © Disney Enterprises, Inc.

Attractions like "California Screamin' " and "Grizzly River Run" quickly won the hearts of many Disney fans, and the exciting simulated hang-glider attraction, "Soarin' Over California", was so popular that it debuted at the Walt Disney World Resort a few years later. "The Twilight Zone Tower of Terror™," a supernatural themed thrill ride, opened to rave reviews in 2004 and towers over the park at 183 feet. Not only the tallest building at the resort, it is the tallest building in the city of Anaheim.

As a combination haunted attraction and free-fall tower, "The Twilight Zone Tower of Terror™" quickly became one of the park's most popular attractions. © Disney Enterprises, Inc.

Guests familiar with the famous Mulholland Drive in Los Angeles will enjoy a laugh on the equally winding "Mulholland Madness, presented by Alamo." © Disney Enterprises, Inc.

For those seeking a white water rafting adventure along the foothills of the Sierra Nevada, "Grizzly River Run" is a must-see attraction. © Disney Enterprises, Inc.

In 2007, The Walt Disney Company announced plans for a billion-dollar revamping of California Adventure—almost twice the cost of its original construction. By June of 2008, the park opened "Toy Story Mania!", a unique attraction, with 3-D effects themed to classic midway-style games. "Walt Disney Imagineering Blue Sky Cellar," an exhibit that opened late in 2008, lets guests get a glimpse of coming attractions set to open during 2010 to 2012. *Cars Land*, a major expansion of the park, is scheduled to open in 2012. It will feature headline rides, including "Radiator Springs Racers," a revamped version of the popular "Test Track" attraction at the Walt Disney World Resort.

From *A Bug's Land* to "Pixar Play Parade," "Turtle Talk" to "Toy Story Mania!," many Disney/Pixar characters have found new homes in Disney's California Adventure Park. Mike and Sulley from "Monsters, Inc. Mike and Sulley to the Rescue!" will soon be joined by Lightning McQueen and Mater when *Cars Land* opens in 2012. © Disney Enterprises, Inc./Pixar

Debuting in the summer of 2008, "Toy Story Mania!" was one of Walt Disney Imagineering's most technologically sophisticated attractions built to date. Unlike other shooting attractions, riders wear 3-D glasses to give the illusion that they are actually throwing darts, pies, or rings at moving targets. © Disney Enterprises, Inc./Pixar

This beautiful Southern California theme park, just steps from Disneyland Park and the excitement of *Downtown Disney*, has a bright future. Just as Walt Disney said Disneyland would never be finished, visitors to California Adventure can expect innovation and surprises for years to come. Disney's California Adventure is sure to remain a favorite destination of both residents and visitors to the Golden State.

Outside the park, guests have almost limitless shopping, dining, and entertainment options in *Downtown Disney,* which was added to the resort in 2001 with Disney's California Adventure Park. © Disney Enterprises, Inc.

With a unique set of attractions and many more in the works, Disney's California Adventure Park has already become a time-tested landmark for the best of California entertainment. © Disney Enterprises, Inc.

8 Funderland

Sacramento, California

Located in California's capital city, Sacramento, Funderland is California's northernmost amusement park. An essential part of the 166-acre William Land Park, this tiny amusement park shares its neighborhood with the Sacramento Zoo, a golf course, and Fairytale Town—a small children's area where fairytale stories come to life. Though Fairytale Town and the Sacramento Zoo are often linked with Funderland, the amusement park maintains its own identity as a must-see for anyone with children under the age of ten.

In the early 1940s, Raymond Silva opened a small park on Funderland's present site called Land Park Kiddie Land. In 1947, there were a small collection of children's rides, including a carousel and "Oscar the Fish"—both of which are still in operation today. During the carousel's opening week, over 6,000 children took an initiating ride on the attraction, and the carousel still maintains its popularity with children of Sacramento over sixty years later.

The entrance gate to California's northernmost amusement park.

A park original, "Oscar the Fish," has been entertaining visitors since 1947 and is still a popular ride with the park's youngest visitors

The beautifully maintained 1940's Allan Herschell Carousel is still a centerpiece attraction at Funderland.

Raymond Silva operated the rides in this park until 1978, when he passed the park to his daughter, Raylin. She continued his traditions for five years, until 1983, and sold the rides to an amusement park and carnival enthusiast, Sam Johnston. Wasting no time on his newest park, Johnston had the two-acre site fenced for the safety of the children and the entire park was landscaped. As a courtesy to nearby residents, he also constructed a sound wall around the site to muffle the laughing and shrieking sounds of delighted children. By the early 1990s, Johnston had built the rest of the park's current rides, including a family roller coaster and a children's log flume that wound through miniature sets and shady, green trees.

Without any large hills and a maximum weight of 200 lbs. per log, "Log Flume" is child-friendly take on the classic theme park ride.

Funderland's "Dragon Coaster" is a mild roller coaster suitable for the entire family.

Funderland itself is a tiny park but it plays an important role in the much larger William Land Park it calls home. Revenue helps to support the nearby Fairytale Town and Sacramento Zoo and provide improvements for the surrounding area in general. Those who visit William Land Park know it is a place for the whole family and a haven from the surrounding capital buildings of Sacramento. With attractions for any age, including a golf course, William Land Park provides something for everyone and makes a gorgeous place to lay down a picnic blanket after a few hours at Funderland.

Not surprisingly, the park has become a popular place to hold birthday parties for young children. Funderland's lack of large rides keeps it a charismatic family place; the park provides a safe and engaging environment for parents to bring their children and have fun together. Today, as always, eager children wait outside with their parents for the park to open. Grasping at the gate and rushing in when finally unlocked, Sacramento children understand Funderland's charm, which is sure to keep this park popular for years come.

Circling the entire park, the "Funderland Train" is a great attraction to begin the day or relax on after a picnic.

The log flume's next-door-neighbor, "Back Road Buggies," shares a few thematic miniature sets with the water ride. Guests can enjoy a scenic and shady ride on both attractions.

A quaint birthday patio at Funderland shows why the park has become a popular place to hold a child's birthday party.

9 Gilroy Gardens
Gilroy, California

Gilroy Gardens is California's only horticultural theme park. It has been a runner-up for *Amusement Today*'s worldwide "Best Landscaping" award for the past several years. Gilroy Gardens' natural and organic beauty is a serene reminder that a family park can effectively combine fun with creative landscaping to invent a whole new experience. Formerly known as Bonfante Gardens, this park was opened in 2001 by Michael and Claudia Bonfante, the owners of Nob Hill foods. Their mission, to inspire families to better understand and appreciate nature, was a dream 25-years in development and finally realized. Best known for its world famous Circus Trees with caricature branches bent into complex and laughingly obscure designs, the Gilroy Gardens preserve and display nineteen of the remaining twenty-five trees developed by Axel Erlandson in the 1920s. Featured in Ripley's *Believe It or Not* in the 1940s and 1950s, Erlandson's botanical expertise remains a mystery to many who admire these living sculptures. It is quite a challenge to comprehend the process behind their intricate formations throughout the park.

Axel Erlandson's famous "Basket Tree" now grows in Gilroy Gardens. With multiple connected tree trunks, Erlandson's creation is actually several trees that have grown into one.

The "Sky Trail Monorail" offers a bird's-eye view of the *Monarch Garden*'s greenhouse. One of the park's six specialty gardens, it offers three viewing levels, each of which yields a uniquely different experience.

Guests need to keep a sharp eye if they hope to spot all nineteen circus trees on display at the park. If they don't, they may find themselves walking past—or through—the trees without even realizing it.

The entrance to Gilroy Gardens offers a clue why the park is considered one of the most exquisitely landscaped in the world.

The park features two family roller coasters along with six unique rides inspired by local agriculture. Among these include the giant "Mushroom Swing," the "Artichoke Dip," and of course the "Garlic Twirl"—a tribute to Gilroy's fame as the "Garlic capital of the world." Other fun and entertaining attractions include a diverse selection of exciting family-friendly rides, awe inspiring plant exhibits, and educational gazebos. Swishing paddle boats, a massive rock maze, and half a dozen specialty gardens display endless varieties of elaborate and unusual plants and foliage. The park's newest addition, the *Splash Garden* complete with water-park attractions and an exhilarating waterslide, sits prominently above the park's major lake inviting guests and families to cool off from a warm California summer day.

The "Quicksilver Express Mine Coaster" is a scenic roller coaster that winds through a thematic mining camp and, of course, almost 600 trees.

Guests can enjoy paddle-boating through scenic Coyote Lake. Behind, visitors can take a ride on the park's giant "Mushroom Swing."

Gilroy Gardens offers education and amusement in a nontraditional way, and caters to families with young children. The peace and tranquility in the park creates a unique and enjoyable experience for its guests, and in few other theme parks will patrons find such serenity. While enjoying the "Panoramic Wheel" in the afternoon, there is little sound but the birds and distant laughter of families in the *Splash Garden*. As a result, the whole experience is memorable not only as entertainment, but also as a place to "get away from it all." Even without the rides, the botanical ensembles alone are enough to spark the interest of nature fans for years to come.

Instead of teacups, riders can enjoy a spin in a garlic bulb at this horticultural theme park.

The smaller of the two coasters, "Timber Twister" snakes through the scenery on a serpentine express.

Whether spinning around in a garlic bulb or watching a show with animatronic vegetables, driving through the south county backroads or floating through the *Rainbow Garden*, there is opportunity for new experience everywhere. Gilroy Gardens will continue to impress, inspire, and teach families not only about the wonder and beauty of nature but the importance of letting imaginations grow in this one-of-a-kind experience.

Another of the park's gardens, the *Rainbow Garden*, is best traversed by raft.

Five waterfalls at *Bonfante Falls* offer a great way to cool off in the afternoon.

Outside, the "Sky Trail Monorail" offers a meandering path through the park's treetops.

The park offers so many isolated areas that any guest can find solace at Gilroy Gardens.

10 Knott's Berry Farm

Buena Park, California

Few parks anywhere in the world have as rich a history as Knott's Berry Farm. As America's first theme park, Knott's was original in creating a scenic setting for guests rather than offering only rides. This wildly popular and historic park began, as the name suggests, as a berry farm.

In the 1920s, Walter Knott and his family sold berries and pies from a roadside stand beside state Route 39. In the 1930s, a friend, Rudolph Boysen, introduced the Knotts to a strange new berry he had crossbred from a blackberry, a raspberry, and a loganberry. Unfortunately, Boysen was unable to keep the new breed alive, as the berries died on the vine. Because he was a seasoned berry farmer, Knott took the new vines and nurtured them to health. They proved to be an instant hit at Knott's stand. When asked what they were called, he proclaimed "Boysenberries."

Like most people in America, the Knotts struggled to make ends meet during the Great Depression. Mrs. Knott opened their house to guests passing along Route 39 and served all-inclusive chicken dinners with a slice of Boysenberry pie for dessert. As Southern California developed, Route 39 became the major thruway between Los Angeles and Orange County, and word spread about Mrs. Knott's famous fried chicken dinners. Soon, lines of hungry people extended for hours outside the farmhouse. To keep the guests entertained, Mr. Knott relocated buildings from old ghost towns in Arizona and California to his property creating an extravagant and authentic ghost town. Today, the ghost town is the most famous section of the park and it is credited as the beginning of America's first theme park.

Knott's Berry Farm's first themed land, *Ghost Town*, has been around since 1940 and is credited as the beginning of the historic park. As the sign depicts, guests are transported back to 1885 once they enter.

The park pays attention to little details in its attractions—especially in *Ghost Town*. There, guests are invited to pan for gold and observe a local blacksmith shaping tools.

"The Gun Shop" in *Ghost Town* is a replica of a building from the California gold rush town of Angels Camp in the 1850s.

Before guests even pass through the park gates, they get a taste of the thrills that await them at America's first theme park.

Walter Knott continued to add to the park through the decades, growing it from what he once dubbed a "summer-long county fair," complete with Boysenberry pie eating contests, into a major theme park with the expansion of land, attractions, and rides. By the 1970s, the park showcased three lands: the original *Ghost Town*, *Fiesta Village*, and *Roaring '20s*, each highlighting important events in American history. In October of 1973, Knott's Berry Farm introduced its now-famous, haunted, Halloween event, *Knott's Scary Farm*. In 1975, the park made history when it opened "Corkscrew," the world's first modern-day roller coaster to take riders upside-down in a 360°, corkscrew roll. Since then, the park has claimed other firsts, including "Xcelerator" in 2002 (the world's first hydraulic launch coaster) and in 2007 "Sierra Sidewinder," America's first free-spinning, multiple-car-train roller coaster. The park's award-winning *Camp Snoopy* offers fun for the young crowd. While many of the older attractions, such as the "Calico Mine Ride" and "Timber Mountain Log Ride" offer incredible journeys that recall California's Old West history.

The entrance to *Camp Snoopy*, a very popular attraction for children.

"Xcelerator," the world's first hydraulic-launch coaster, has an intimidating personality but is one of Knott's most exciting rides.

In the past few years, Knott's has added some of the world's best coasters to its park.

"Perilous Plunge," the world's tallest and steepest water ride when it opened in 2000, is a popular attraction mid-summer for obvious reasons. Standing 115 feet tall, the ride is just 34 feet shorter than the real Niagara Falls.

Daily transportation by stagecoach is still a part of Knott's Old West charm. Knott's historic "Timber Mountain Log Ride" was one of the first log flume attractions in the United States. The ride offers an incredible themed journey through a 19th century logging camp.

The "Pony Express," a coaster added in 2008, has guests sit as though they were riding a horse.

At over 250 feet tall, "Supreme Scream" offers a tremendous bird's-eye view of the park and of Los Angeles. Some even say they can see the Disneyland Resort from the top before plummeting back to earth at more than 50 mph.

As America's first theme park, Knott's Berry Farm, inspired an entire industry. Its thrilling rides and themed lands have made it world famous, yet it retains its nostalgic roots and guests can still sample that famous fried chicken dinner and Boysenberry pie.

After a long day at Knott's Berry Farm, there is no better way to unwind than with one of Mrs. Knott's famous fried chicken dinners and, of course, a slice of the pie that built America's first theme park.

11 LEGOLAND California

Carlsbad, California

A relative newcomer among California theme parks, LEGOLAND California opened March 20th, 1999. This cheerful park celebrates the colorful miniature building bricks so popular with children, and for several consecutive years has been named "World's Best Children's Park" by trade newspaper *Amusement Today*. The third LEGOLAND Park, out of four currently in existence, LEGOLAND California is the only one that does not call Europe "home." The LEGO Company, based in Denmark, opened its first theme park in its native country in 1968 and followed several decades later with the remaining three. Appropriately, "lego"—or "leg godt"—means "play good" in Danish.

Hollywood, or "LEGOWOOD," is popular in *Miniland*'s Southern California exhibit.

LEGOLAND California has quickly become the world's most popular children's park.

Many sites throughout LEGOLAND are constructed with actual Legos.

Legoland California is both a family ride park and an exhibition of LEGO miniatures. *Miniland USA*, one of the nine exciting themed lands that make up the park, offers some of the world's most exquisitely detailed miniatures featuring major cities and locations throughout the United States. Constructed with more than 24 million LEGOS, *Miniland USA* comprises the majority of the 40 million little bricks found throughout the park. Depicting seven geographical areas of the country, including New York City, Las Vegas, and the California Coast, the attention to detail is astounding. Everything from the exact location of hotels along "The Strip" in Vegas to the army of animated yellow taxi cabs at Times Square, is meticulously recreated on a "1-to-20" scale.

The New York City skyline is enough to make even the tallest guest look up.

Florida's Daytona Beach is an interactive LEGO mini-display where guests can race mini-dragsters.

Eight more themed lands await guests alongside *Miniland USA,* including the newest, *Land of Adventure*, where fortune-hunters of all ages can explore Egypt by searching through hidden tombs for treasure on the park's first dark ride, "Lost Kingdom Adventure." A shooting attraction through a secretive pyramid tomb, LEGOLAND arms its guests with state-of-the-art laser guns for a rugged, all-terrain adventure that is lit with black light.

The entrance to "Lost Kingdom Adventure", LEGOLAND California's first dark ride, features a towering, 16-foot-tall Egyptian Pharaoh made with more than 300,000 of the popular building bricks.

LEGO-themed rollercoasters, LEGO-themed boat rides, and even a LEGO-themed spinning teacup attraction, seen here, make for inventive experiences that entertain the imaginations of all children who visit.

Targets are illuminated by blue lights in LEGOLAND's shooting attraction, "Lost Kingdom Adventure." Those with the best aim receive the highest score.

Children are welcome to imagine and explore their way through the additional lands, including *Pirate Shores*, a land heavily built around water attractions; *Castle Hill*, a medieval romp with damsels and dragons; and *Dino Island*, a prehistoric venture.

For any young engineers-in-training, a tour of the on-site LEGO factory is also a must. Bright little bricks are pressed hot off the assembly line as children are walked through the steps of creating everyone's favorite building brick. The Big Shop, LEGOLAND California's premier souvenir store, has the largest selection of LEGO products and LEGO sets found anywhere in the nation, giving kids the chance to take home, along with their memories, actual pieces of this amazing park.

The "Coast Cruise" gives guests the opportunity to see world-famous constructs assembled with LEGOS. The Taj Mahal and Mount Rushmore are just two of the many destinations visited.

Elvis Presley, among others, graces the LEGOLAND "Block of Fame."

All parks face heavy competition for the title of "World's Best," and LEGOLAND lives up to the honor. It is a park that offers something for all children and all families: from awe at the park's Brontosaurus that is assembled with more than two million LEGOS to excitement from a ride on the park's Coastersaurus. Those who grew up playing with LEGOS—and those who still do—will find surprise and delight at this amazing theme park.

The "LEGO Factory Tour" takes guests through the step-by-step process used in creating LEGOS. For inquisitive guests, this short attraction is a must.

A glimpse of LEGO Chinatown in *Miniland USA*. LEGOLAND employs an army of LEGO engineers to keep the *Miniland USA* sets pristine. Great attention to even the smallest details are what makes this unique park so special.

12 Pacific Park

Santa Monica, California

Historic Route 66 is arguably the most famous highway in the United States. Still often referred to as "The Mother Road" or "Main Street USA," it was once the most popular route between Chicago and Los Angeles. For the traveler heading west, Pacific Park on the Santa Monica Pier still serves as the glorious oceanfront finish line that juts out 1600 feet into the sea.

The Santa Monica Pier opened on September 9th, 1909, offering visitors a novelty walk above the Pacific Ocean. Rides on the pier came along a few years later when a merry-go-round and roller coaster were added, the beginnings of an amusement park. As a whole, Pacific Park is one of the few surviving reminders of a time many refer to as the "Golden Age" of amusement parks. The park's monumental Hippodrome building from 1916, which still houses an antique carousel, has since been dedicated a National Historic Landmark. Pacific Park also has the distinction of being the only west coast amusement park still operating on a pier.

The city of Santa Monica as seen from the pier. On a sunny summer day, the beach is often Pacific Park's most popular attraction.

Traveling the length of the Santa Monica Pier at 35 mph while passing a variety of boardwalk games and attractions along the way, "West Coaster" offers a great way to tour the park with spectacular ocean views the entire time.

A frequenter of Pacific Park sits atop his lofty perch.

In addition to the spectacular beach and Pacific Park's variety of games and attractions, guests can enjoy fishing, street performers, and often even live music on the Santa Monica Pier.

The park's bright beginning was later followed by hard times. By the 1930s, the park's popularity had declined, precipitating the closure of the roller coaster, and in the 1950s a change in ownership. The pier was in such poor condition in the 1970s that the Santa Monica City Council ordered its demolition. Immediately, residents of Santa Monica campaigned to save their tired, but beloved, landmark. Their dream was realized when construction began on a new concrete substructure to add strength and stability to the pier. New rides, retail stores, restaurants, and entertainment transformed the park and pier into a newly popular destination. Today, Pacific Park on the Santa Monica Pier is an emblem of California, and it makes frequent appearances in nation-wide televison commercials and hit movies, due in large part to its close proximity to Hollywood.

Many local merchants pedal their specialty wares on the pier, making it a great place to find unique figurines, art, and clothing.

The carousel and Hippodrome building still draw an ample amount of guests looking for a bit of seaside nostalgia at the Santa Monica pier.

In addition to twenty classic boardwalk games, guests can find a state-of-the-art arcade at Pacific Park as well.

A whimsically designed octopus welcomes guests to the west coast's only amusement park still operating on a pier.

Popular restaurants, like the Bubba Gump Shrimp Co., make the Santa Monica Pier not only a great place for amusement but for dining as well.

In addition to the spectacular beach setting, twelve rides attract visitors to Pacific Park. The giant "Pacific Wheel," an enormous solar-powered Ferris wheel, complete with thousands of multi-colored lights, illuminates the coastline every evening. The park's lone roller coaster, "West Coaster" provides a panoramic view of the beaches curving from Marina del Rey to Malibu, while cars glide around the perimeter of the pier. And what seaside park would be complete without bumper cars? Guests can find them and other family rides, plus more than twenty classic midway games and even a modest-sized aquarium, on the pier.

"West Coaster" gives guests the opportunity for a truly breathtaking view while circling 55 feet above the pier.

A century after it opened, visitors continue to flock to the amusements on the Santa Monica Pier, eager to experience the history, nostalgia, and fun of Pacific Park. Public sentiment preserved it and its fans will keep the big wheel turning under the stars for years to come. Like Historic Route 66, the park is a treasure to remember and a hallmark of the Golden State.

Two Pacific Park attractions, "Sea Dragon" and the park's iconic "Pacific Wheel."

The last shop on the pier marks the end of Route 66. There, guests can find their souvenir t-shirt to commemorate the trip.

13 Pixieland Amusement Park

Concord, California

Tucked away in a quiet corner, nestled inconspicuously between a duck pond and little league baseball field, is the miniature Pixieland Park. Driving by, one could easily miss it, since Pixieland boasts none of the flashy signage typical of most attention-grabbing theme parks. Instead, the park's unique charm lies hidden to most, behind clusters of large, shady trees. For those who know where to look, however, this little park is a wonderful find.

Pixieland Park has been around for over fifty years, and local residents with young children make up the "park regulars." It was built in the late 1950s by toystore-owner Norman Rosenburg, and was originally called King Norman's Wonderland. The park opened with a merry-go-round, Ferris wheel, train, and miniature cars that required a driver's license issued by the park.

Like the popular car ride originally offered at King Norman's Wonderland, every child has the opportunity to drive through the scenic and well-kept track at 5 mph.

With benches and galloping horses, all family members can enjoy the carousel, regardless of age.

Through the Pixieland gates lies a carnival of fun for young visitors.

The park's ensemble of rides hasn't expanded much over the past half century though the park has since added a family roller coaster, a family free-fall attraction, and a few others. Limited in size, the park's inability to expand actually adds to its appeal because the park caters to families with young children between the ages of two and seven. Parents don't have to worry about losing their kids in the typical theme park setting—the entire park is visible from any point within.

Pixieland Park was closed for a short time in the mid-1960s, as many carnival-style parks of its size died out to make room for the up-and-coming theme park giants. However, the allure of this park kept it alive, as a former employee, Bill Edwards, bought the rides and moved them briefly to Oakland. By 1970, Pixieland was restored to Willow Pass Park in Concord, where it has remained to this day.

Like the rest of the park, every ride is suitable for small children, even the dragon roller coaster.

The "Frog Hopper" is a miniature free-fall attraction perfect for any young thrill-seeker. Parents may find this ride surprisingly more exciting than it looks, should they choose to ride.

It seems fitting that the park was built by a toy store owner, as Pixieland seems to be a toy store come to life. Rides that feature little trains, cars, and airplanes appear to have been plucked off a nursery shelf and make the experience not only exciting for kids but a great lesson in imagination as well. It's no surprise that the park often hosts children's birthday parties with old-fashioned balloons, clowns and a prize booth. The park is geared toward kids that aren't yet ready to spend an entire day at a theme park and would be much more affable to just a few hours.

Pixieland captures the imaginations of young children and creates an immersive and carnival-style amusement park exclusively for those seven or younger. Reminiscent of a time when little theme parks spanned the state, Pixieland keeps this charming portion of California history alive. To some loyal guests, bigger would never be better—the welcoming family environment is more than enough of a draw. Assuming the park will continue to avoid the trend toward faster and more exciting rides, Pixieland will be around for many more years, offering family memories to all its young guests.

An express train offers guests a grand tour of the park and surrounding area.

One of the Pixieland's toystore-looking planes offers visitors a peaceful flight over the park.

The miniature car ride winds past several child-sized homes, including the gingerbread house seen here.

14 Rotary Storyland and Playland

Fresno, California

Compared with the rest of the state, California's Central Valley offers few amusement parks. In fact, Fresno's Rotary Storyland and Playland parks are more than 100 miles from their nearest neighbor, Gilroy Gardens. While they stand apart, these parks also stand out as an example of selfless community spirit and service. A combined family amusement park and children's fairytale village, Rotary Storyland and Playland makes a visit to Fresno worthwhile for anyone with children under the age of ten.

The park's history dates back to the mid-1950s when Dr. Joe Logan, president of the North Fresno Rotary Club from 1954-1955, got the idea for a family amusement park on the city's ninety-acre Roeding Park. Like the Rotary Club, a national non-denominational service guild that acts on the motto "service above self," this park opened as a non-profit organization and has remained so for the more than fifty years. Funds from the park flow back to the Fresno Park Department, which provides upkeep of additional park facilities in the city. Since the 1950s, Rotary Storyland and Playland has contributed well over two million dollars to the Fresno community.

Once the afternoon warms up in California's Central Valley, *Playland*'s water play area becomes a popular attraction for park guests of all ages.

Side by side, the "Little Rocko" Ferris wheel attraction offers a great substitute for younger guests who don't quite meet the height requirements for "Big Rocko."

The park's smallest guests can enjoy picnicking on a toadstool in a wooded area near "Alice's Court."

When the park opened on May 30, 1955 there was no *Storyland*, just a small collection of rides called "Rotary Playland." *Playland* was an instant success and has flourished through the decades with an assortment of nine rides. *Storyland*, a walk-thru park dedicated to fantasy and fairy tales opened in 1962. However, the park struggled to maintain the steady income *Playland* enjoyed, and by 1994 faced the prospect of closing its gates for the last time. Fortunately, Rotary Playland donated $100,000, and a merger of the two parks kept *Storyland* afloat. Today, both parks—now often billed as one—are important features of local history to the Rotary Club, the city of Fresno, and California's Central Valley.

The dragon roller coaster, one of the nine rides offered at *Playland*, is a family ride that children and parents can enjoy together.

At the far end of the park, guests can find "King Arthur's Castle," one of more than twenty storybook sets in the park's *Storyland*.

The round table and throne are inside "King Arthur's Castle."

Jack and Jill take a tumble down a hill.

Little Boy Blue rests under one of Roeding Park's many shady trees in *Storyland*.

Playland's newest attraction, pirate-themed paddle boats offer gorgeous views of adjacent Lake Washington. A small train travels the lake's edge uniting the parks with a pleasant journey among trees, through tunnels, and past ducks and geese that live peacefully on the lake's island. Storyland offers a literacy field trip program to encourage young children to learn about the fun of reading. Also, taking a page from Children's Fairyland in Oakland, it uses the same "Magic Key" system invented by Fairyland for all its interactive fairytale displays and playgrounds.

The whole of Roeding Park includes the Fresno Chaffee Zoo (helped tremendously by donations from Playland), picnic areas, tennis courts, horseshoe pits, and wide, grassy, lakeside fields. Truly a California park gem, the Rotary Storyland and Playland tradition of "service above self" will continue to improve the city of Fresno and grow young minds in a way that only California's most altruistic theme park can.

At *Playland*'s "Shipwreck Cove" boat dock, guests can take a paddle boat around an island on the miniature Lake Washington.

The "Willis B. Kyle Express Train" rounds Lake Washington to complete its short journey and deliver guests from *Playland* to *Storyland*.

Humpty Dumpty before his great fall. Guests may recognize the talking storybook and magic key system invented by Children's Fairyland available throughout *Storyland*.

A weathered sign near *Storyland*'s entrance describes the philanthropic mission of the park. "No profit has been sought, no credit desired, just the happiness of children of all ages who enjoy this Storyland of Fresno."

15 Santa Cruz Beach Boardwalk

Santa Cruz, California

In 1907, half a century before Disneyland and a decade before World War I, President Teddy Roosevelt was in the White House as the Santa Cruz Beach Boardwalk opened. This charming seaside park is the oldest in California and has remained a timeless monument to a bygone era. It combines the tradition of yesteryear with the best of new-age technology; there is something special about this landmark. As one of the few remaining seaside parks that was operating during the 1920s' Golden Age of amusement parks, this old boardwalk was voted the "World's Best Seaside Amusement Park" for the past several years by trade newspaper *Amusement Today*.

Guests find spectacular shopping along the boardwalk to meet all of their Santa Cruz beach-going needs. In addition, they can satisfy their sweet tooth with salt-water taffy and candy apples from Marini's, a candy store that has been in business since 1915—almost as long as the Boardwalk itself.

As one of the oldest amusement parks in the world, the Santa Cruz Beach Boardwalk has played an important role in preserving seaside park nostalgia. This "Laffing Sal," from the long-since-closed Playland at the Beach amusement park in San Francisco, has a new home at the boardwalk in Santa Cruz.

All guests can find a nostalgic experience at the world's most popular seaside amusement park.

Envisioned as "The Coney Island of the West" by its creator, Fred Swanton, the Santa Cruz Beach Boardwalk has truly withstood the test of time. While other seaside parks succumbed to fires, the Great Depression, and changing tastes in entertainment, this Boardwalk has endured. In 1987, its 1924 Giant Dipper roller coaster and 1911 Looff Carousel were dedicated National Historic Landmarks for their contribution in shaping America. However, while memories of the "Golden Age" can still be found in every corner of the park—which has preserved its past as faithfully as a museum—the Boardwalk is no stranger to the innovation that continues within the industry. Attractions like the interactive "Desperados" western theater keep the park young and always on the horizon of new entertainment.

Though the National Historic Landmark "Giant Dipper" is one of the ten oldest coasters in the world. It continues to be voted one of the world's twenty-five most popular wooden coasters.

"Desperados" has guests ride mechanical saddles and wagons while rounding up bandits with a posse in the Old West.

Along with its three roller coasters and log flume, the park offers many family rides such as bumper cars, and its gorgeous ocean view can be enjoyed night and day from atop the Ferris wheel, the thrilling "Double Shot!" or the "Skyglider." The Boardwalk's classic 1911 Looff Carousel still uses the original 1894 Ruth & Sohn organ, as well as its nostalgic brass ring dispenser, so riders can take aim at a large clown mural on the far wall; riders who toss a ring into the clown's mouth set off a heady array of lights, sirens, and whistles as they continue to triumphantly circle.

Standing 125 feet tall, guests cannot find a more spectacular ocean view than from the top of the park's "Double Shot!"

Still in pristine condition, this 1912 Wurlitzer Organ continues to delight and impress carousel riders of all ages alongside the carousel's original 1894 Ruth & Sohn organ (not pictured).

A rider reaches for a brass ring on the park's National Historic Landmark "Looff Carousel."

The Boardwalk immerses visitors in a sense of history, nostalgia, and old-fashioned fun. With its century old carnival style games and old fashioned snack booths, the park is a living example of the county fairs that were once the season highlight of any small town. Over the years, the Boardwalk has also hosted countless beachfront events, from swimming and surfing exhibitions to state beauty pageants. During the summer months, the park puts on a free beach concert series featuring prominent modern artists and big names from the past, which appropriately celebrates both the old and the new.

In addition to its impressive ensemble of rides and classic boardwalk games, the park also features countless arcades. From the latest innovations in video game entertainment to the park's "classic corner," featuring Pong, Pac Man, and Centipede, among others, the boardwalk blends the old and new here, as it does so successfully everywhere else in the park. The arcades expand to include multiple prize centers, a shooting gallery, and even an enormous laser tag arena, seen here.

The Santa Cruz Beach Boardwalk is a treasure to experience and remember. It continues to offer thrills, romance, and family fun, as well as a glimpse of life in another time. As an older couple dances in the sand to a song they loved half a century ago, a young teen couple sits shyly on the bleachers together for the first time; some things never change in this small coastal town, even after more than a century.

This two-story, incredibly themed, pirate miniature golf course is one more attraction offered by the park in its countless arcades.

The "Hurricane" roller-coaster offers the best—and most thrilling—seat to watch beach concerts during the summer.

Guests visiting the boardwalk have literally a mile-long beach to spend their day in the sun.

16

Scandia Amusement Park

Ontario, California

Many children across California are familiar with the name Scandia. In the Golden State, the name is almost synonymous with the words "graduation night" or "birthday." It therefore comes as no surprise that Scandia is not the name of just one location, but several scattered liberally across California and Nevada. However, those familiar with the Scandia chain would argue it is hard to classify Scandia's self-titled Family Fun Centers as full-blown amusement or theme parks. Scandia Amusement Park, in Ontario, California, is a recent opening of the chain and the only one that deserves such distinction.

The Scandia chain began when the first location opened in Sacramento in June of 1976. At the time, this family fun center consisted of two miniature golf courses and a 4,000-square-foot video arcade. Later, baseball batting cages, go-carts, and bumper boats were added, all staples of future Scandia family fun centers. In 1979, the second Scandia center opened, in Fairfield, California, southwest of Sacramento. Another at Las Vegas, Nevada, followed in 1985 and one more at Victorville, California, in 1988.

Ontario's Scandia Amusement Park opened in 1992, the first park to include coasters and a modest ride park, in addition to the core attractions offered at the other Scandia locations. In 1995 the large "Scandia Screamer Coaster" as well as the more child-friendly "Little Dipper Coaster" were unveiled.

The first hill gives a hint why Scandia's main coaster is appropriately named the "Scandia Screamer Coaster."

No Scandia family fun center would be complete without go-carts. The "Stockholm Raceway" provides an exciting thrill ride in addition to the "Screamer."

With clubs in hand, two excited patrons make their way out of the Scandinavian castle toward the miniature golf courses.

The owners' Scandinavian heritage was impetus for the park's name, theme and decor which include hand-built replicas throughout the miniature golf courses of actual mansions, churches, and other buildings found in Scandinavia. All rides in the park, such as the "Stockholm Raceway" and "Baltic Sea Bumper Boats," are either named after landmarks or people from the region. Classic rides, like the "Viking Ship" and "Olga's Tilt-A-Whirl" take on signature flair of the Northern-European themed park transforming what could easily be misconstrued as a small carnival into a cozy family experience. Milder children's rides, like the "Copenhagen Carousel" and "Oslo Fire Dept." round out the theme park into something everyone will enjoy.

The bumper boats prior to setting sail on the park's Baltic Sea.

Guests play around a miniature Scandinavian fishing dock on one of the golf courses.

The "Denmark Railway" offers a mild and scenic ride under the tracks of the Scandia "Screamer."

Scandia Amusement Park embodies a more subdued and relaxed atmosphere than the other parks in Southern California. Because it is smaller, it doesn't consume an entire day like most others. A game or two on the mini-golf courses and a ride on the roller coaster can make the perfect family outing.

Scandia's success has not only helped its owners realize a unique American dream in family fun centers, it has enabled them to give back to their community. In the past 30 years, Scandia has donated millions of dollars to charities and value-based organizations. Additionally, the owners are engaged in running an orphanage in Mexico and supporting Christian missionaries. Scandia is an amazing success story, and the chain is generously sharing its good fortune throughout the world.

Thanks to an abundance of trees, golfers remain shaded from the park's hot afternoon sun for the duration of their time on the courses.

Guests choose from 150 games in the park's arcade—enough to hold any guests' interest, even without rides.

17 SeaWorld San Diego

San Diego, California

Minutes inland from beautiful San Diego beaches is one of the world's most popular marine life parks. SeaWorld San Diego, the first of the famous SeaWorld chain of theme parks, saw great success when it opened in 1964 as a marine zoological park. It quickly gained renown for its awe-inspiring shows and attractions themed around water and aquatic life.

SeaWorld was the brainchild of four U.C.L.A. graduates in the early 1960s. Originally they dreamed of building an underwater restaurant with a complementary marine-life show, but over time that idea developed into plans for a marine-life theme park. Marine-life parks at that time were rare to nonexistent, so when SeaWorld opened with a modest collection of dolphins, sea lions, and other sea creatures, it was an instant hit. Curious and fascinated patrons filled the park to witness, enjoy, and learn about rarely studied animals. Since then, the park has expanded its variety of aquatic life and was the first park in the world to feature orca whales when it added them in the late 1960s. Over the years, SeaWorld San Diego has become home to pilot and beluga whales, penguins, sharks, seals, and many other aquatic creatures.

"Shamu," one of the park's resident killer whales, splashes the audience during SeaWorld San Diego's show, "Believe." Photo used courtesy of SeaWorld.

SeaWorld's aquariums feature more than 5,700 fish, representing more than 400 species, including moon jellyfish. Photo used courtesy of SeaWorld.

A rose anemone moves with the current at "Aquarium de la Mer" while its companion, a starry rockfish, keeps one wary eye toward guests. Photo used courtesy of SeaWorld.

High-flying dolphins and pilot whales entertain and amaze at SeaWorld San Diego. Photo used courtesy of SeaWorld.

While the park has built a reputation around its prominent marine life collection, it also has added several world-class rides in recent years. "Journey to Atlantis," which opened in 2004, is a combination boat ride and rollercoaster with intricate theming and stunning audio-visual effects. The attraction takes riders through a narrated legend behind the Lost City of Atlantis, and combines the best of flume drops and coaster turns with an indoor simulated underwater portion. This self-proclaimed "future of thrill rides" is an experience unlike any other in California. Additionally, the rides "Shipwreck Rapids," a river rafting attraction, and "Wild Arctic Ride", an arctic-themed simulator, place special emphasis on water-themed elements.

"Journey To Atlantis" is SeaWorld San Diego's thrilling water coaster, featuring twists, turns, and a splashy, 60-foot plunge. Photo used courtesy of SeaWorld.

Adventurers enjoy a wet and wild ride on SeaWorld San Diego's "Shipwreck Rapids." Photo used courtesy of SeaWorld.

In 2008, SeaWorld welcomed Sesame Street into the theme park with the opening of *Sesame Street Bay of Play*, a new area especially for children. A new 4-D show hosted by Elmo and friends helps round the park with plenty of family friendly entertainment.

Younger guests will enjoy a ride on "Elmo's Flying Fish." Photo used courtesy of SeaWorld.

Sesame Street Bay of Play at SeaWorld is a two-acre, whimsical play area that features family-friendly attractions, including "Abby's Sea Star Spin." Photo used courtesy of SeaWorld.

Marine life education is a main goal of the park, and each day children are invited to take part in feeding sessions with the seals and dolphins. SeaWorld works to promote wildlife conservation and preservation, and its scientists and zoologists provide valuable research on marine life and endangered species.

SeaWorld San Diego's popularity has multiplied, like Disneyland, beyond California, but this is the place that started it all. Marine animals, spectacular shows, and now rides are all in one place—this park is absolutely unique in the Golden State.

Polar bears dive and swim at SeaWorld San Diego's "Wild Arctic," an attraction that features a simulated jet helicopter ride and exhibits with polar bears, beluga whales, walruses, and seals. Photo used courtesy of SeaWorld.

Rescued and rehabilitated manatees gently glide through their 800-square-foot habitat at SeaWorld San Diego. Photo used courtesy of SeaWorld.

Antarctic penguins, including Emperors, waddle inside SeaWorld San Diego's 25-degree "Penguin Encounter." Photo used courtesy of SeaWorld.

At SeaWorld San Diego's "Forbidden Reef," moray eels swim in their underground cavern. Up above, the exhibit also features graceful bat rays that glide by in a shallow lagoon. Photo used courtesy of SeaWorld.

18 Six Flags Discovery Kingdom

Vallejo, California

Situated just a little northeast of the San Francisco Bay in Vallejo, Six Flags Discovery Kingdom has the largest and most diverse collection of animals of any theme park in the state. With attractions that correspond to the park's three themes—Land, Sea, and Sky—Six Flags Discovery Kingdom offers a trio of fun and entertainment that is suitable for guests of any age.

The park has had an interesting history throughout the years. It originally opened in Redwood City in 1968 as an oceanarium called "Marine World." After several years, the Marine World aquarium merged with a struggling animal park called "Africa USA" and was renamed "Marine World/Africa USA." In 1986, the park relocated to Vallejo and over a decade later, opened its new season with rides, coasters and other attractions again changing its name, to "The New Marine World Theme Park." The following year, the park was purchased by the Six Flags chain and again renamed "Six Flags Marine World"; it wasn't until 2007 that the park became "Six Flags Discovery Kingdom."

Guests can—literally—come face-to-face with some interesting characters at "Six Flags Discovery Kingdom."

A local Discovery Kingdom resident enjoys the sunny California weather. For those interested in learning more about all types of wildlife, the park offers a variety of park safaris and educational programs to its guests.

All guests will enjoy the beauty of the "Butterfly Exhibit." Those that do visit, however, must be sure to check their clothes upon leaving; a few of the garden's inhabitants have been known to hitch a ride out of the greenhouse on unsuspecting guests.

In addition to world-class Six Flags coasters, guests can find an incredible menagerie of wildlife at this animal-themed park.

Six Flags Discovery Kingdom has been expanding with new coasters on an almost regular basis since 1997. Currently, the park offers eight roller coasters, including "Medusa," "V2: Vertical Velocity," and the newest, called "Tony Hawk's Big Spin." When "Medusa" opened in 2000, it was the first floorless roller coaster on the west coast and featured the world's tallest vertical loop at 128 feet. In addition, the ride also introduced the world's first "sea serpent roll," a type of roller coaster maneuver that has since been copied by steel roller coasters across the globe. "Vertical Velocity," also known as "V2," came along shortly after, and is California's only spiraling impulse coaster—a type of coaster that launches riders backward and forward up vertical towers several times.

The "Medusa" roller coaster amid its now-famous "sea serpent roll." Behind is the ride's notorious, 128-foot, vertical loop.

"Boomerang" was the park's first rollercoaster in 1997.

In 2002, the park's close proximity to a nearby airport brought trouble with the building codes; no coaster in the park was permitted to exceed a height of 150 feet. "Vertical Velocity" was well over that height. To comply with the regulation, the front tower of the coaster was modified from 90° to 45° making it the first and only spiraling impulse coaster in the world to launch at 45°, although completely by accident. "Tony Hawk's Big Spin," a skatepark themed "spinning roller coaster" added in 2008, seems to be a testament that Six Flags Discovery Kingdom will continue to seek new ways to excite and thrill its guests in the future.

Though the front tower was modified to a spiraling 45° angle, the back tower of "V2: Vertical Velocity" continues to launch guests backward and straight up, at 70 mph.

Cars on "Tony Hawk's Big Spin" rotate on a separate axis than the coaster track; thus, where guests choose to sit dramatically affects the experience of every rider in the car. Should two heavy riders sit across from two lightweight riders, the car will spin more intensely.

Though to many guests the coasters are enough of a draw, there are plenty of children's and family attractions as well. *Looney Tunes Seaport*, *Tava's Jungleland*, and *Thomas Town* (themed after the well-known Thomas the Tank Engine) keep the little ones entertained. And true to its "Marine World" and "Africa USA" roots, the park also offers a killer whale and shark experience as well as elephants, birds, and lizards that make Six Flags Discovery Kingdom an adventure for the whole family with its land, sea, and sky attractions.

In the "Shark Experience," guests can get up close with oceanic carnivores. Here, a sawfish rests on the sandy floor.

Thomas Town is popular with the park's younger crowd.

A cougar awakens from his siesta at "Cougar Rocks."

Guests begin their climb up the lift hill on Discovery Kingdom's "Kong" roller coaster.

19 Six Flags Magic Mountain

Valencia, California

For big coasters, there is no comparison to Six Flags Magic Mountain. Opened on May 29, 1971, by Newhall Land and Farming Co., the park was built as a more thrilling alternative to Knott's Berry Farm and Disneyland. Since then, the park has revolutionized the coaster industry by being locked into a never-ending battle to be the park with the most coasters in the world. As of 2010, this park offers sixteen different roller coasters, which will keep any coaster enthusiast enthralled for their entire visit.

In 1976, Magic Mountain began its coaster revolution—quite literally—with the opening of the famed "Great American Revolution." Eight days before "Corkscrew" opened at Cedar Point in Ohio, Magic Mountain debuted "Revolution" as the first modern coaster ever to feature a 360° vertical loop. A name play on the bicentennial year and on the effect it would have on the future of coaster possibility, the ride showcased operators dressed in historic revolutionary war uniforms. In 2002, the American Coaster Enthusiasts commemorated the ride as a "Coaster Landmark" with a plaque viewable up in the park's "Sky Tower."

The "Revolution" continues to thrill riders, as it always has since 1976.

Although it does not see as many riders as it did in its heyday, the "Revolution" remains an important piece of history for this acclaimed park.

Since Magic Mountain opened in 1971, it has contributed much to the coaster world. From the world's first "revolutionary" vertical loop, seen here (white track), to its new-age counterpart—the incredible flying coaster "Tatsu" (orange track), the park has always operated on the cutting-edge of roller coaster thrills.

Since 1976, this park has continued to bring the latest and greatest coaster technology to all its rides. In 1978 it brought "Colossus," one of the world's tallest coasters at the time and still the tallest wooden coaster in the West. In 1979, the same year Six Flags bought Magic Mountain, "Roaring Rapids" was brought to the park. A river-rafting ride that is now at home in many parks across the state, it was the first of its kind on the West Coast when it opened. "Ninja, The Black Belt of Coasters" was introduced in 1988 as the West Coast's first suspended-swing coaster, and it is still billed as the world's fastest suspended coaster. In the late 1990s, two more landmarks appeared: "Superman: The Escape" and "The Riddler's Revenge." "Superman" opened as the world's tallest and fastest roller coaster of all time, and was the first to reach a speed of more than 100 mph during the ride. "The Riddler's Revenge," from 1998, still holds bragging rights as the world's tallest, fastest, and longest standing coaster (it is a "standing" coaster, meaning you stand up while riding it), a distinction still "standing" to date.

Atop Six Flags Magic Mountain sits "Superman: The Escape." Prior to boarding the ride, guests first travel into Superman's Fortress of Solitude. As an "arctic" dwelling, it remains heavily air-conditioned, a welcoming thought to most guests who have to climb several hills in the sun to reach the landmark attraction.

"The Riddler's Revenge" appropriately competes with "Batman: The Ride" for the most riders, in the uppermost section of the park.

No trip to *Gotham City* would be complete without a ride on "Batman: The Ride."

A glimpse of the park's *Gotham City Backlot*.

The new millennium at Six Flags Magic Mountain has already seen some of the most spectacular coasters in history. "Goliath," an 85-mph steel ride featuring a 255-foot drop into a small underground tunnel boasted the longest and fastest drop of any complete-circuit coaster in the world at its opening. "Tatsu," the world's tallest, longest, and fastest flying coaster ever, opened in 2006 followed in 2008 with the reopening of "X" as "X2," the world's first "5th dimensional coaster" with seats on a separate axis from the track and an all-new sensory experience of visual and audio effects. With the 2009 opening of "TERMINATOR® SALVATION: THE RIDE," it seems safe to assume there are many great coasters still in store for this pioneer of thrills.

As the world's tallest, fastest, and longest flying coaster ever built, "Tatsu" is an electrifying attraction that actually gives its riders the perception of flight.

Although it does not feature any flips or inversions, "Goliath" is one the park's most popular rides.

"X2" features seats capable of spinning on a separate axis than the coaster itself, while the combining audio and visual effects provide a complete sensory experience.

With the addition of *Thomas Town* and *Bugs Bunny World*, this park is moving toward more family entertainment and attractions for all ages. But when it comes to the best in coasters, there is still no place like Six Flags Magic Mountain.

As seen from the park's "Sky Tower," cars from both "X2" (background) and "Viper" (foreground) make their way up the initial launch hills.

In addition to being the world's fastest ride ever, at its opening in 1997, "Superman: The Escape" was also the tallest, at 415 feet.

20 Universal Studios Hollywood

Universal City, California

A theme park born from the glitz and glamour of mid-century Hollywood, Universal Studios has become an icon of the Southern California experience—an astounding theme park with emblematic and star-studded roots. As one of the oldest and most famous Hollywood studios still in use, Universal has found a way to transport every guest past the velvet ropes and onto the red carpet during their visit to the Studios.

Universal Studios Hollywood did not start as a theme park; it was a place to make movies—a working Hollywood studio. Initially the studio offered a modest tour of sets and soundstages. There were no rides and nothing that would resemble the modern theme park of today. However, in 1962, when MCA (Music Corporation of America) took over Universal Pictures, things began to change. In 1964, the modest tour expanded, offering the first ride of a new theme park, the world famous "Studio Tour" (formerly known as Glamortram). Still operating today, it is the park's most famous attraction, offering a 45-minute tour through actual television and movie sets and Hollywood backlots. Many Hollywood movie tricks and stunts are shown first-hand during the ride.

Guests are encouraged to begin their day with the world famous "Studio Tour," still the park's most popular attraction.

Authentic movie props and sets are visible throughout the park, such as this one from Apollo 13.

The Universal globe, at the entrance of the park, has become a symbol of world-class entertainment and an icon of Universal Studios.

Since then, Universal Studios Hollywood has added more rides including "The Simpsons Ride™," a state-of-the-art version of a classic simulator. The experience begins as soon as the guest enters the line; while patrons wait in the queue, the Simpsons characters also queue up on video screens, making the normal wait for an attraction a unique and even essential part of the experience.

While waiting in line at "The Simpsons Ride™," guests can buy snacks from Simpsons' Kwik-E-Mart owner, Apu, or buy a Duff Beer from Simpsons' bartender, Moe, two recent hires at "Krustyland."

"The Simpsons Ride™" is one of the most technologically advanced in California. The attraction begins with a visit to Springfield's newest amusement park, "Krustyland."

"Jurassic Park®– The Ride" offers the latest technology in a water ride. With authentic stages from the movie transported to Universal Studios Hollywood exclusively for the ride, it is a one-of-a-kind experience that puts guests right into the movie. Traversing a jungle laden with prehistoric beasts, the boat journeys through the blockbuster movie, ending in a very close encounter with a T-Rex and an 84-foot soaking vertical drop. "Revenge of the Mummy℠– The Ride," an indoor psychological coaster, also presents movie theming at its best. Speeding through the darkness, backwards and forwards, chased and shadowed by the supernatural, Revenge of the Mummy is a coaster all in its own league.

The technology and setting of "Jurassic Park®– The Ride" culminate in a visually stunning result.

All rides at Universal Studios Hollywood feature incredible scenery, from beginning to end. Walking through the gates of "Jurassic Park®– The Ride," guests are immediately transported into the 1993 Spielberg film.

In terms of entertainment, Universal Studios Hollywood is unrivaled with amazing shows and spectacular effects. From "Shrek 4-D™" and "Backdraft" to "Special Effects Stages" and "Universal's House of Horrors," the park offers the best of today's movie technology. With the "Adventures of Curious George" water play area, kids and kids at heart will always have something to fit their taste at any moment. The glitz and glamour of old Hollywood is still very much alive; Universal Studios will continue to preserve it and offer an exciting experience beyond the velvet rope.

Guests meander down one of the park's themed walkways.

A series of lengthy escalators bridge the two lands of the park, *Upper Lot* and *Lower Lot*.

Once the day begins to heat up, "The Adventures of Curious George" becomes a very popular attraction.

For those with a bit more daring and nerve, the walk through the "House of Horrors" features famous horror movie villains from every era of Hollywood history.

Every day, the park welcomes thousands who come to experience world-class entertainment and leave with the satisfaction of a day of red-carpet treatment.

Timeline
1907 100+ years and counting...
The Santa Cruz Beach Boardwalk, California's oldest amusement park, opens.
1959 Thrills Become Themed
Disneyland introduces storytelling to thrill rides with the Matterhorn Bobsleds.
1958 One Revolutionary Sore Throat
Bruce Sedley's world famous "Talking Storybooks" are added to Children's Fairyland.
1924 Let the Thrills Begin!
The Giant Dipper, California's oldest roller coaster, opens at the Santa Cruz Beach Boardwalk.
1955 A Legacy Begins...
Disneyland opens and forever change theme park industry.
1956 Milestones and Muppets
The Children's Fairyland Puppet Theater, oldest continuously operating puppet theaterin the country, parts its curtains for the first time. Frank Oz begins his puppetry career.
1932 The Berry That Built an Empire...
Walter Knott introduces the world to the first Boysenberry.
1925 Botanical Breakthroughs
Axel Erlandson begins developing Circus Trees that found a home at Gilroy Gardens 80 years later.

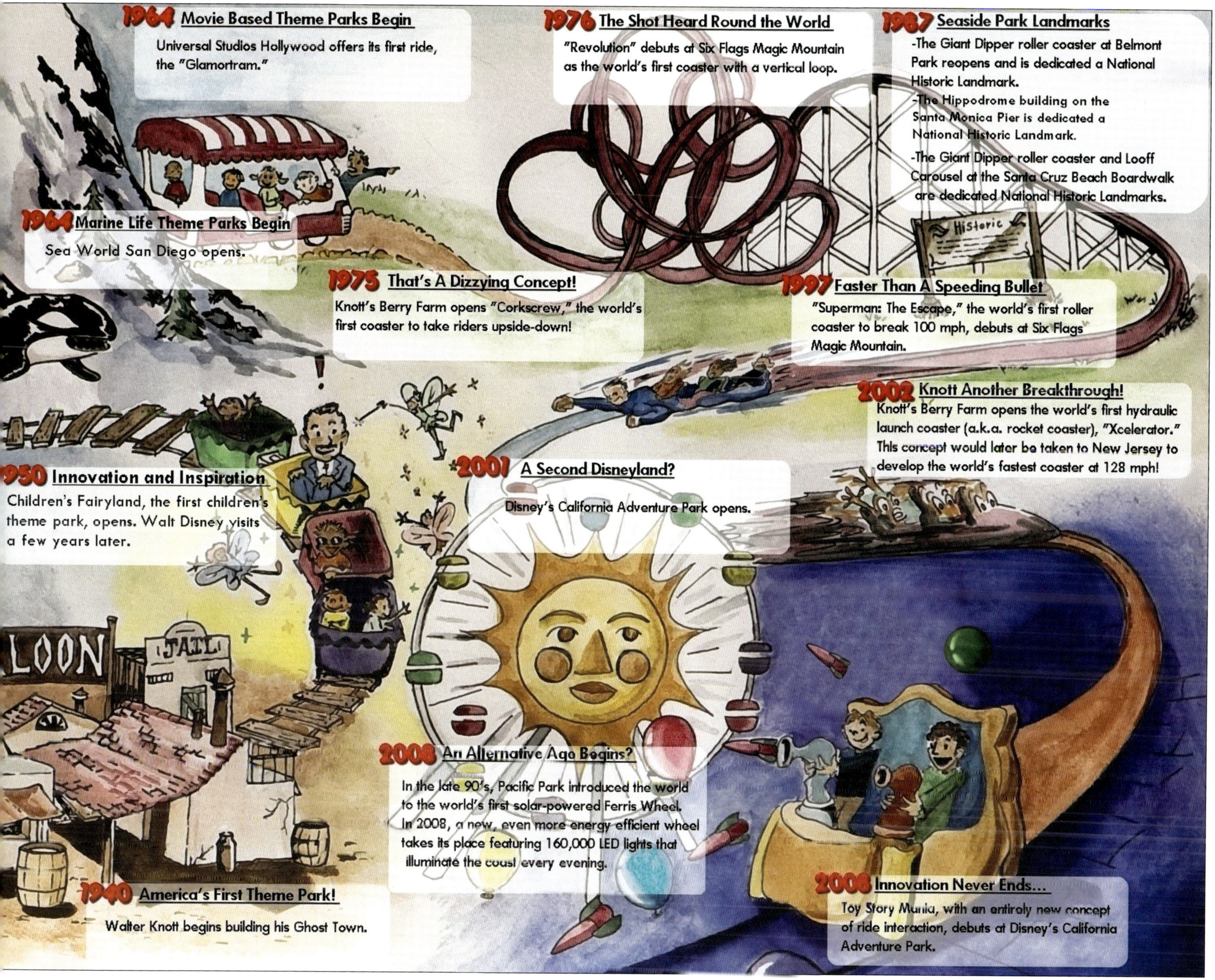

1940 America's First Theme Park!

Walter Knott begins building his Ghost Town.

1950 Innovation and Inspiration

Children's Fairyland, the first children's theme park, opens. Walt Disney visits a few years later.

1964 Movie Based Theme Parks Begin

Universal Studios Hollywood offers its first ride, the "Glamortram."

1964 Marine Life Theme Parks Begin

Sea World San Diego opens.

1975 That's A Dizzying Concept!

Knott's Berry Farm opens "Corkscrew," the world's first coaster to take riders upside-down!

1976 The Shot Heard Round the World

"Revolution" debuts at Six Flags Magic Mountain as the world's first coaster with a vertical loop.

1987 Seaside Park Landmarks

-The Giant Dipper roller coaster at Belmont Park reopens and is dedicated a National Historic Landmark.

-The Hippodrome building on the Santa Monica Pier is dedicated a National Historic Landmark.

-The Giant Dipper roller coaster and Looff Carousel at the Santa Cruz Beach Boardwalk are dedicated National Historic Landmarks.

1997 Faster Than A Speeding Bullet

"Superman: The Escape," the world's first roller coaster to break 100 mph, debuts at Six Flags Magic Mountain.

2001 A Second Disneyland?

Disney's California Adventure Park opens.

2002 Knott Another Breakthrough!

Knott's Berry Farm opens the world's first hydraulic launch coaster (a.k.a. rocket coaster), "Xcelerator." This concept would later be taken to New Jersey to develop the world's fastest coaster at 128 mph!

2008 An Alternative Age Begins?

In the late 90's, Pacific Park introduced the world to the world's first solar-powered Ferris Wheel. In 2008, a new, even more energy efficient wheel takes its place featuring 160,000 LED lights that illuminate the coast every evening.

2008 Innovation Never Ends...

Toy Story Mania, with an entirely new concept of ride interaction, debuts at Disney's California Adventure Park.